Fabulous Farm

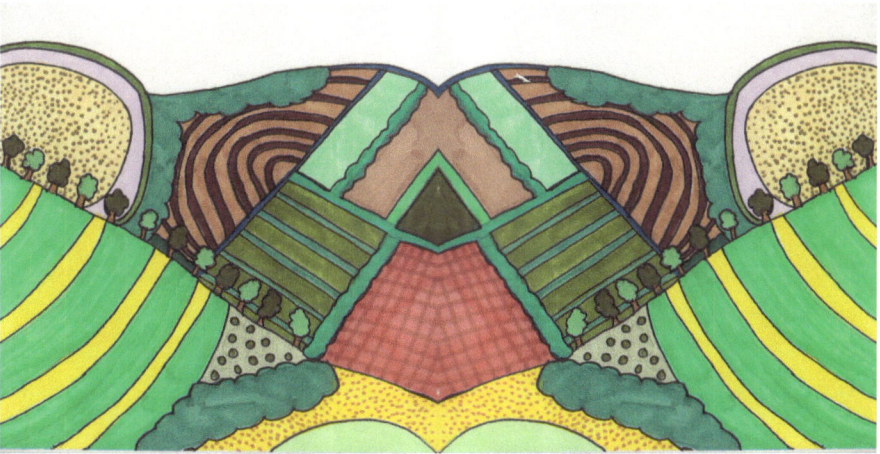

Hadley James

Fabulous Farm

Hadley James

Contents

Good Morning

Sun is up,
Cockeral crows,
Animals wake,
Off he goes!

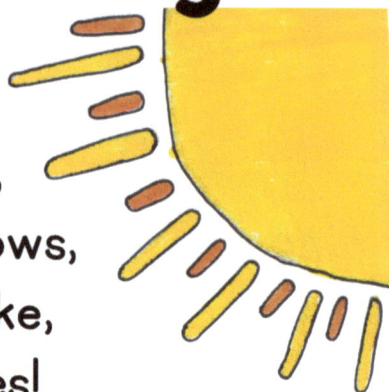

Pigs snuffle,
Farmers yawn,
Everyone's up,
At the crack of dawn.

Hens cluck,
Dogs bark,
Birds all sing,
With the lark.

Sheep baa,
Ducks quack,
Hungry geese,
Have a snack.

Horses neigh,
Cows moo,
Everyone welcomes
The day that's new.

Rise and Shine

Early in the morning,
When the sun begins to rise,
The farmer jumps straight out of bed,
And rubs his weary eyes.

He stumbles down the stairs,
And makes a cup of tea,
Then he gets to thinking,
About the day that's going to be.

He has a little breakfast,
Puts on his boots and coat,
Then goes into the farmyard,
To check up on the goat.

He feeds the goat and says hello,
Then moves on to see the hens,
He opens up their house,
And lets them out into their den.

Next stop is the stable,
It's nice and warm inside,
He pets all the horses,
but has no time for a ride.

The last stop is the cowshed,
It's nearly milking time,
The cows are getting ready,
Stood in a tidy line.

The morning rounds are over,
The farm's up and alive,
There's still much more to do today,
And it's only just past five!

Cock-a-Doodle-Doo

As the dawn is breaking,
When the day is new,
I have a very special,
Important job to do.

I wake up with the sunrise,
Then I get to work,
I am everyone's alarm clock,
To help them feel alert.

I start to sing my song,
I cock-a-doodle-doo,
To tell everyone it's morning,
And it's time to get up too!

I stand so very proud,
My feathers red and gold,
I'm welcoming the day,
In my way so loud and bold!

Not everybody likes me,
They say cock-a-doodle-don't!
But I will keep on singing,
I just can't stop - I won't!

Hens

We live in our house together,
One big happy family,
When it's time to go out in the morning,
We're as happy as can be.

We like to explore the farmyard,
Inside and outside our home,
We like to dig for grubs and worms,
The world is ours to roam.

We have lots of fun in the farmyard,
We like to have baths in the dust,
We even like to roost in the trees,
For some of us it is a must.

When it gets a little darker,
And it's time to say goodnight,
We snuggle down in our hen house,
Until the first morning light.

Cat

I'm queen of the farm,
Yes, that is me!
Nothing happens around here,
That I do not see!

I keep an eye on the ducks,
And watch all the hens,
And purr at the pigs,
As they roll in their pens.

I look after the farmhouse,
And lap up the cream,
Then chase all the mice,
My life is a dream!

Dog

I wake up with the boss,
And get ready to start the day,
I have a little breakfast,
But there's no time to play.

We go out into the farmyard,
To check everyone's alright,
They are all still sleepy,
As it is not yet light.

I have a little bark,
To tell them all I'm here,
And that I will protect them,
So there's nothing to fear.

When we go up to the field,
Then it's my turn for fun,
I look after the sheep,
And run and run and run.

When it is evening,
And I'm starting to tire,
I eat my yummy dinner,
Then curl up by the fire.

Sheep

Out in the fields,
Day after day,
Munching the grass,
Watching the lambs play.

Out with the flock,
We all stick together,
We're there for each other,
Whatever the weather!

Chickens

Peck, peck, peck,
We scratch at the ground,
Peck, peck, peck,
There are treats to be found.

Peck, peck, peck,
We're hunting for treasure,
Peck, peck, cluck,
It's our greatest pleasure.

Peck, cluck, cluck,
We bathe in the dust,
Peck, cluck, cluck,
Keeping clean is a must.

Cluck, cluck, cluck,
We go back to our home,
Cluck, cluck, cluck,
Tomorrow we'll roam!

Cows

In the field,
On a sunny day,
We're with our heard,
And eat, rest and play.

We chew the grass,
For hours and hours,
But always take time,
To smell the flowers.

We like to sit down,
And have a rest,
With other cows,
That we like the best.

Don't forget,
That you will find,
We will remember,
If you are unkind!

Goat

I love to climb,
All over the place,
Even up trees,
I think climbing is ace!

I'm very curious,
I like to explore,
All around me,
There's excitement galore!

I like to eat,
Grass, hay, and weeds,
I also like kitchen scraps,
Grains and seeds.

I have beautiful horns,
Hooves and a beard,
And just like a sheep,
I sometimes get sheared!

Geese

Honk! Honk!

We love our pond,

We're a big family,

With a very strong bond.

Honk! Honk!

We love to fly,

Our V formation,

Will catch your eye.

Honk! Honk!

We're birds of a feather,

Whatever the weather,

We'll flock together.

Donkey

Hee haw! I love to call,
And bray to all my friends,
When we get together,
Our singing never ends!

I like it when it's sunny,
And I'm in the field all day,
But when it's cold and wet,
I just want to hide away.

I love to munch on carrots,
But don't like to be alone,
When I'm with my friends,
Then I really feel at home!

Llama Glama

Hello darling, I'm a llama,
The most glamorous one on the farm,
With my beautiful long eyelashes,
I ooze style and charm.

I like to live with my friends,
We call our group a herd,
We hum to one another,
To talk without saying a word.

If I'm the only llama,
I'll make friends with the goats and the sheep,
I'll take good care of all of them,
And guard them while they sleep.

I don't like lots of drama,
It's not something I seek,
It's good when there's no problama,
And we all have a positive week!

Alpaca

I live in a herd with my friends,
We like to munch the grass,
Some people think we're llamas,
But we have much more class.

I'm small and very furry,
My fur is nice to stroke,
We have 52 different colours,
I promise – it's no joke!

The farmer likes my wool,
It's soft and nice to wear,
It's funny to think of clothes,
Just made out of my hair!

Horses

We love being in the field,
Running wild and free,
But we like to see our owner,
When it's time for tea.

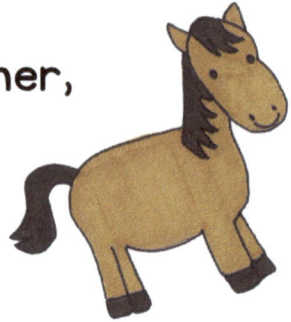

We like to graze and skip,
We like jumping too,
We'll even let you stroke us,
For a sugar lump or two!

Sometimes we can be shy,
And then we want to hide,
But if we know you're friendly,
We'll take you for a ride

Our shoes are very special,
They can bring good luck too,
When we get our new ones,
We will save some just for you!

Tractor

Big and strong,
Heavy and tall,
Riding high,
Above them all.

Ploughing the fields,
Planting the seeds,
Tilling the soil,
And pulling out weeds.

Spreading the muck,
Harvesting crops,
You do it all,
And we think you rock!

Tractor o tractor,
You're such a good friend,
With so many uses,
There's really no end.

Planting Time

The fields are ready,
The seeds are ready too,
The farmer's working hard,
There's a huge job to do.

The seeds and plants are ready,
To be put in the ground,
Let's hope conditions will be right,
To grow crops safe and sound.

The tractor's working hard,
Planting in neat rows,
Now for sun and water,
And let's just hope it grows.

Lambing Time

It's springtime again,
The sun is about,
The lambs are getting ready,
It's time for them to be out!

The sheep are in the pens,
They know just what to do,
Then before you know it,
The lambs are here for you!

They gallop in the fields,
They jump in the sun,
But when they feel scared,
They run straight back to Mum!

Orchard

Trees stand tall,
In orderly rows,
Down in the orchard,
Where the fruit grows.

Apple, plum, peach,
Cherry and pear,
Grow in the sunshine,
And the fresh air.

When they are ripe,
We get ready to pick,
To get the best fruit,
We have to be quick!

Harvest

Golden crops,
Tall and strong,
Waiting for the farmer,
To come along.
Bursting fields,
With seeds sown,
Ripe and tasty,
Vegetables grown.
Food is gathered,
Such a treat,
Tasty things,
For us to eat!

The Farmhouse

Smoke swirls from the chimney,
It's cosy and warm inside,
Dog sits by the fire,
The wind makes him want to hide.

There's a pot upon the stove,
And scorching tea in mugs,
Woolly, snuggly jumpers,
Feel like a squishy hug.

There's a lamb in the living room,
Lying in a pen,
We'll feed her in a minute,
Inside her little den.

The cat stalks round the kitchen,
Looking for a tasty treat,
She's waiting for the milk,
Her favourite thing to eat.

The goat peeps through the window,
He's chewing on the flowers,
Mum will be so cross,
Growing them took hours!

The wind outside is howling,
But we're all safe and warm,
The work is finished for today,
But we'll start again at dawn.

Duck Pond

At the back of the farm,
A lake, calm and still,
It's my favourite place,
To sit, relax, and chill.

I love to watch the ducks,
With their dabbling wiggle,
And when they quack and waddle,
It really makes me giggle.

The swans are elegant,
They look so graceful and serene,
But they're paddling like crazy,
It just can't be seen.

The geese honk and cackle,
They have a funny song,
Sometimes they like to chase me,
We don't always get along!

I love it by the duck pond,
I like to dip my feet,
And watch the world go by,
It feels like such a treat.

Types of Farms

There are different types of farms,
That you will often see,
Each one does a different thing,
Just for you and me.

Pastoral farms have animals,
They might make milk, cheese, and meat,
They take care of the animals,
And give us lovely things to eat.

Arable farms grow crops,
Vegetables and wheat,
And barley, oats, and beans,
For a delicious, tasty treat.

Some farms are a mixture,
They have animals and crops,
They give us lots of produce,
And fill shelves in the shops.

There are lots of different farms,
And lots of food for me and you,
We are thankful for our farmers,
And everything they do.

Thank You

For getting up before it's light,
For working in the rain,
For working so hard all year round,
We want to say again ...

Thank you to our farmers,
Thank you for all you do,
Thank you for the food we eat,
A huge thank you to you!

For planting and sowing,
For looking after crops,
For caring for animals,
We think you are tops.

Thank you to our farmers,
Thank you for all you do,
Thank you for the food we eat,
A huge thank you to you!

For stocking up our shelves,
For helping us make cakes,
For milk and meat and cheese,
And lovely things we bake.

Thank you to our farmers,
Thank you for all you do,
Thank you for the food we eat,
A huge thank you to you!

Also by Hadley James:

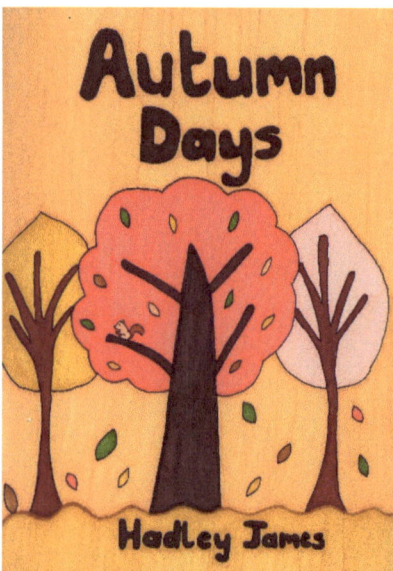

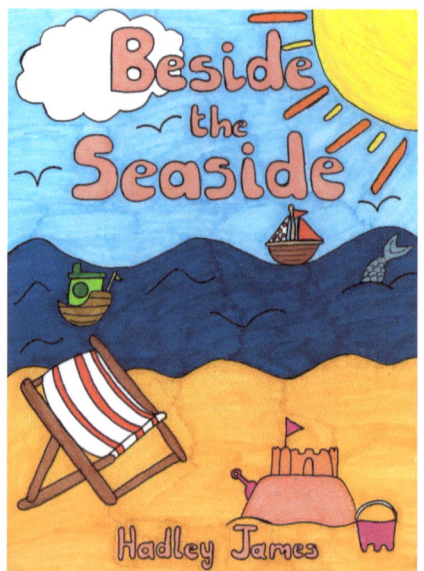

Wonderful Me
Hadley James

Horrid Halloween
Hadley James

Autumn Days
Hadley James

Beside the Seaside
Hadley James

Wonderful Winter
Hadley James

Spectacular Spring
Hadley James

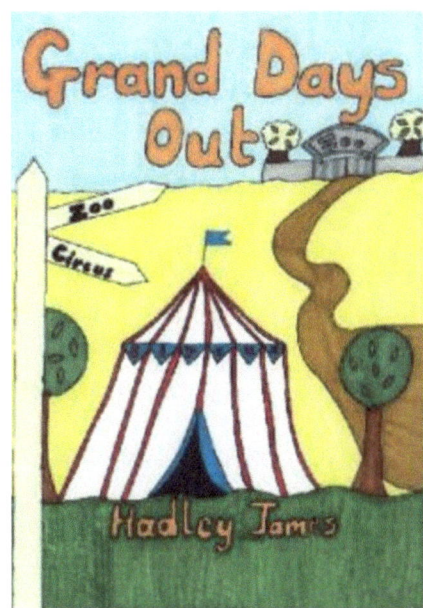
Grand Days Out
Zoo
Circus
Hadley James

Extreme Environments
Hadley James

Summer Dreams

Hadley James

Marvellous Minibeasts

Hadley James

Fabulous Farm

Hadley James

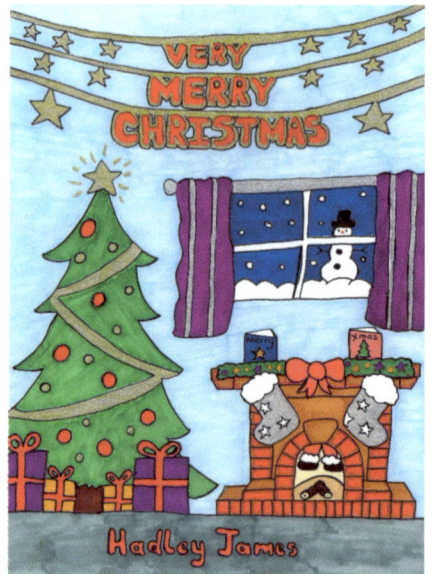

VERY MERRY CHRISTMAS

Hadley James

www.ingramcontent.com/pod-product-compliance
Lightning Source LLC
Chambersburg PA
CBHW040145070426
42448CB00032B/21